snapshot·picture·library

BABY ANIMALS

snapshot · picture · library

BABY ANIMALS

FOG CITY PRESS

Published by Fog City Press,
a division of Weldon Owen Inc.
415 Jackson Street
San Francisco, CA 94111 USA
www.weldonowen.com

WELDON OWEN INC.
Group Publisher, Bonnier Publishing Group John Owen
Chief Executive Officer and President Terry Newell
Senior Vice President, International Sales Stuart Laurence
Vice President, Sales and New Business Development Amy Kaneko
Vice President, Publisher Roger Shaw
Vice President, Creative Director Gaye Allen
Managing Editor, Fog City Press Karen Perez
Assistant Editor Sonia Vallabh
Art Director Kelly Booth
Designer Andreas Schueller
Design Assistant Justin Hallman
Production Director Chris Hemesath
Production Manager Michelle Duggan
Sales Manager Emily Bartle
Color Manager Teri Bell

Text Mariah Bear and Sonia Vallabh
Picture Research Brandi Valenza

A WELDON OWEN PRODUCTION
© 2007 Weldon Owen Inc.

Library of Congress Control Number: 2007936046

ISBN-13: 978-1-74089-989-5

10 9 8 7 6 5 4 3 2
2010 2011 2012

Printed by Tien Wah Press in Singapore.

From the top of a tree to the bottom of the sea, animals are everywhere—and every one of them starts as a baby!

Some hatch out of eggs, and some are born with twelve brothers and sisters. Some hide underground, some in nests, and some in their mothers' pouches.

Watch as baby animals from all over the world snuggle up, eat and play, and start exploring everything around them.

This baby fawn's
white spots
help her hide
in the forest.

But some baby
animals would
rather hide
way up high
in the trees.

These baby foxes
are just the right
color to hide
inside an old log.

When baby
bunnies need
to hide, they
can hop into
their holes.

Many baby
animals are
good at hiding,
because they
are so little.

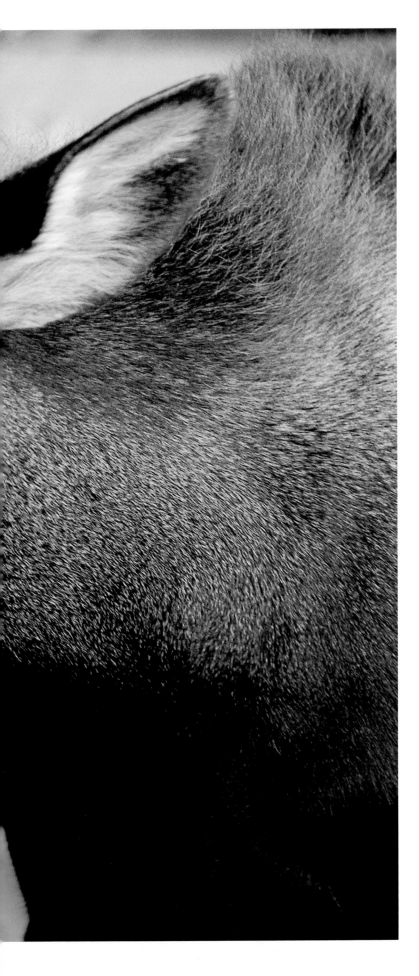

This baby moose may not be all that little, but if he gets scared he can run away on his long legs.

Foals, baby antelopes, and baby alpacas have long legs for running, too.

Baby animals
know that
their best
protection is
to stay close to
their mothers.

Some babies
have no choice!
Baby birds don't
know how to fly
until their parents
teach them.

Mother and
father birds take
turns feeding
their babies
after they hatch
from their eggs.

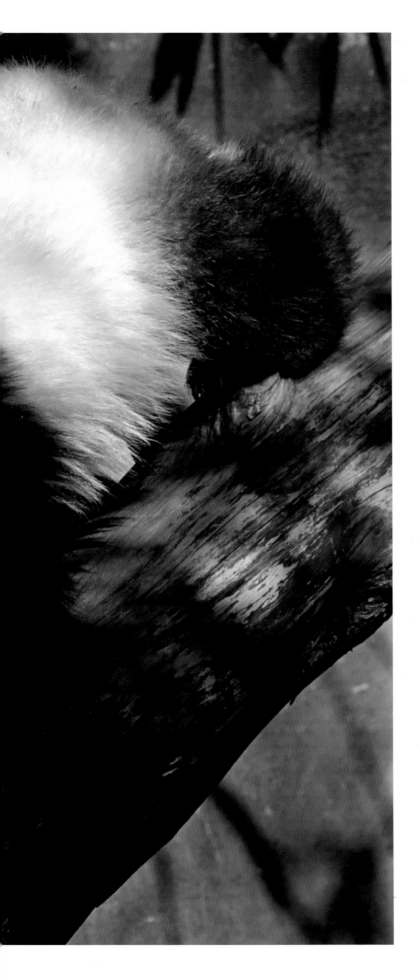

Where is this
panda's mommy?

Here she is!
And here's this
koala's mommy,
too. But where
is this piglet's
mommy?

Baby kangaroos, wallabies, and wombats live in their mommies' pouches. So their mommies are never very far away.

This baby seal
is light gray,
but he will turn
dark gray like the
water when he is
ready to swim.

Orca, beluga, and dolphin babies know how to swim from birth. They spend their life in the water!

Sea turtles hatch on the beach. Like sea lions and penguins they travel far, but they always come home to have their own babies.

A baby crocodile
has to bite his
way out of his egg
using a special
"egg tooth!"

Water dragons, iguanas, and some snakes hatch out of eggs. But other snakes are born like we are.

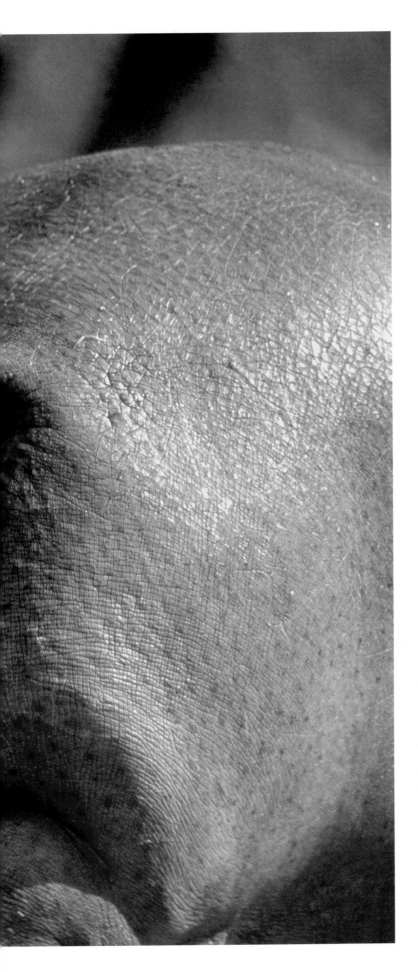

What is this
naughty baby
hippopotamus
up to?

Giraffes, spider monkeys, and zebras usually have only one baby at a time.

But look how many babies this meerkat has! She must be very, very busy!

All baby animals like to play, but soon they come back to snuggle. Just like this ring-tailed lemur…

...and this
baboon and
baby giraffe.

Orangutans live
with their mothers
longer than any
other animal
does...except us!

All baby animals have so much to learn from grown-up animals…

...and so much
to see and
explore!

Better get started!

Chacma
Baboon Infant
Southern Africa

 American Black
Bear Cub
North America

 Cockatiel Chick
Australia

 African
Hedgehog Hoglet
Central Africa

 Gray Wolf Pup
Parts of North
America, Europe,
and Asia

 King Vulture Chick
Southern Mexico to
northern Argentina

 Red-Necked
Wallaby Joey
Australia

 Black-Tailed Prairie
Dog Pup
North America

 Barn Owlet
Worldwide, except
Antarctica

 White-Tailed
Deer Fawn
Parts of the Americas

 Moose Calf
Northern Hemisphere

 Giant Panda Cub
Central and
western China

 Raccoon Kit
North America

 Wild Welsh
Mountain Foal
Wales

 Vietnamese
Pot-Belly Piglet
Vietnam

 American Black
Bear Cub
North America

 Antelope Calf
Europe, Asia, and
Africa

 Giant Panda Cub
Central and
western China

 Squirrel
Monkey Infant
Parts of the Americas

 Alpaca Cria
South America

 Koala Joey
Australia

 Red Fox Kits
North America,
Europe, parts of Asia

 Mute Swan Cygnets
Europe and
western Asia

 Red-Necked
Wallaby Joey
Australia

 Giant Otter Whelp
South America

 Chestnut Welsh Foal
Wales

 Gray
Kangaroo Joey
Australia

 European
Rabbit Leveret
Southern Europe

 Common Piglets
Europe and Asia

 Hairy-Nosed
Wombat Cub
Australia

 European
Rabbit Leveret
Southern Europe

 African Gray
Parrot Chicks
Africa

 Gray Seal Pup
Both shores of the
north Atlantic

Orca Calf
All Oceans

 Hippopotamus Calf
Sub-Saharan Africa

 Nubian Giraffe Calf
Eastern Sudan, northeastern Congo

 Bottlenose Dolphin Calf
All oceans except the Arctic and Antarctic

 Nubian Giraffe Calf
Eastern Sudan, northeastern Congo

 Orangutan Infant
Indonesia, Malaysia

 Beluga Whale Calf
Arctic and Sub-Arctic Oceans

 Squirrel Monkey Infant
Parts of the Americas

 Macaque Infant
Northern Africa and Asia

 Cape Fur Seal Pup
Southern Africa and Australia

 Plains Zebra Foal
Southern and eastern Africa

 African Lion Cub
Africa

 Green Sea Turtle Hatchling
All oceans except the Arctic

 Slender-Tailed Meerkat Kits
Botswana, South Africa

 Wild Piglet
Europe, Asia, and northern Africa

 Emperor Penguin Chick
Antarctica

 Spotted Hyena Whelp
Africa

 Ring-Tailed Lemur Infant
Madagascar

 Freshwater Crocklet
Australia

 Bengal Tiger Cub
India, Southeast Asia

 Red Fox Kit
North America, Europe, parts of Asia

 Water Dragon Hatchling
Southeast Asia and Australia

 Ring-Tailed Lemur Infant
Madagascar

 African Lion Cub
Africa

 Green Tree Python Hatchling
New Guinea, Indonesia, parts of Australia

 Yellow Baboon Infant
Eastern Africa

 Margay Kitten
Central and South America

 Water Dragons
Asia and Australia

 African Lion Cub
Africa

 Mountain Gorilla Infant
Central Africa

ACKNOWLEDGMENTS

Weldon Owen would like to thank the following people for their assistance in the production of this book: Diana Heom, Ashley Martinez, Danielle Parker, Lucie Parker, Phil Paulick, and Erin Zaunbrecher.